WINCHESTER
CASTLE
AND THE GREAT HALL

A CASTLE FOR A CONQUEROR

It was the Romans who first recognized the military and commercial importance of Winchester's site – the place where the River Itchen cuts a routeway through the chalk downs on its journey to the sea. Soon after landing in AD43 they settled there and within 25 years Venta Belgarum, the fifth largest town in Britain, had been created.

To protect their new town they built a wooden (later stone) wall and on the high ground where the castle was later to stand, they made a massive earth rampart, 800 feet (246m) long and 200 feet (61m) wide. A fort was built on top. After the Roman Empire collapsed in the early 5th century, Winchester declined both socially and physically.

Civilized life there only revived during the reign of Alfred (871–99), but by 1066 when William the Conqueror's forces arrived soon after the Battle of Hastings, they were handed control of not only a thriving community, but the seat of the Anglo-Saxon kings and the home of the royal treasure and government records.

Winchester was the focus of great trouble during the reign of Henry I's weak nephew, Stephen (1135–54). Matilda, Henry's daughter, had a strong claim to the throne and from 1139 for '19 long winters' a bitter and destructive war raged. Chroniclers said that 'Christ and his saints slept'.

When Matilda captured Stephen in 1141, Henry de Blois, Bishop of Winchester and Stephen's half-brother, handed over to her the castle and its treasure, including the royal crown. Before long, though, the two fell out. Matilda, based in the castle, laid siege to Bishop Henry in Wolvesey Palace in the city. Stephen's queen then besieged the entire city, which for two months in 1141 suffered severe damage. Finally Matilda was forced to abandon the castle and flee for her life to the west.

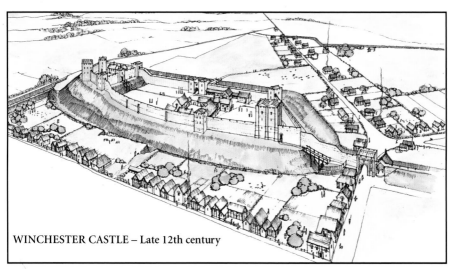

WINCHESTER CASTLE – Late 12th century

LEFT:
Winchester Castle as it was in the reign of Henry II (1154–89). Clearly visible are the defensive salient on which the castle stands, the Norman keep and the newly built Westgate (right) which can still be seen today.

In addition to this, William saw that Winchester would act as a bridgehead against the unconquered people of Mercia to the north. He therefore ordered a castle to be built on the Roman rampart, one of the first Norman castles in Britain. The old Roman wall surrounded it on three sides. On the fourth, facing the city, the Normans dug a ditch and bank, capped by a timber palisade. Within these walls were built the halls and chambers of a palace, which gradually superseded the ancient palace of the Saxon kings down in the city.

Later, King Henry I (1100–35) built a square stone keep to house the royal treasure and the famous Domesday Book, the comprehensive survey of England's property and its ownership. The keep's massive foundations still lie beneath the paving of Castle Yard.

Henry II (1154–89) further fortified and enlarged the castle but, in general, the 12th century saw it become less of a fortress and more a residence. Halls, chapels, gardens and other domestic buildings were added. Amongst these were new chambers for Henry and his wife, Eleanor of Aquitaine, who had an enforced and lengthy stay in the castle during 1173 and 1174 when her sons were first in rebellion against the king.

The castle was neglected in the reign of King John (1199–1216). By the time he died Winchester had for some years been superseded by London in its importance to the Crown. Financial matters were now dealt with in Westminster, where the royal treasure was by that time permanently housed. Winchester Castle had become little more than a royal residence, but under John's son, Henry III (1216–72), it was to have its finest hour.

Henry was the monarch most responsible for making Winchester a fine medieval castle. A great patron of the arts and architecture, he was born and baptized in the city and, as an adult, regularly spent Christmas at the castle with his wife, Eleanor of Provence.

In the year of Henry's accession at the age of nine, the castle was briefly occupied by the French (see panel below). Alarmed by this, the king's advisers made hasty repairs and reinforcements, in particular demolishing the Norman keep, to replace it in 1222 with an imposing round tower on an adjacent site.

In 1216, during struggles between the Barons and the monarchy, the castle was captured by Louis, son of Philip II of France. Two weeks of heavy battering by siege engines made huge breaches in the walls and filled the ditches with the resulting debris.

Having taken the castle, the French made frantic attempts to repair the damage they had done, but in 1217 the castle was recaptured by forces fighting for John's son, the new King Henry III.

GROWTH AND DECLINE

O n coming of age in 1227, Henry III commenced a programme of work on the castle that was to cost £10,000 and last throughout his long reign. The main gate, in the western wall, was rebuilt together with the bridge that led from it across a widened castle ditch. On the other side of the bridge a new two-turret gate was built for additional protection. By 1258 new high towers along the castle's eastern walls dominated the city.

Henry's most significant contribution, as far as we, today, are concerned, was the construction (1222–36) of a new Great Hall. After the earlier hall had been demolished, the larger hall that we see today was erected on a site a few metres nearer to Westgate. In this new hall the sturdy wall at the eastern end formed part of the castle walls.

The year 1302 saw the first of three major setbacks in the castle's history. While Edward I, son and successor to Henry III, was spending Easter at the castle with his wife, Margaret, fire broke out causing such widespread damage to the royal apartments that adequate repair was out of the question. After that, royal visitors usually lodged at Wolvesey Palace, the Bishop's residence, and the castle ceased to hold such personal importance for subsequent monarchs.

Largely because of this, the 200 years that followed saw a great change in the castle's role. As direct links with royalty diminished, the castle gained importance as a legal and administrative centre. From time to time, royal courts and councils of state were held in the Great Hall (25 between 1079 and 1449), and it was here that Crown tenants had to report in order to pay their rents and to renew their oath of allegiance. In this day-to-day business, the castle's long history as the administrative centre for Hampshire's county affairs had its origin.

From the early 16th century, the residential buildings of the medieval castle fell into disuse and dilapidation. Only the Great Hall was regularly maintained because of its legal and administrative functions. After Elizabeth I became Queen in 1558, the Crown handed the castle over to the Winchester city authorities, but while the Great Hall continued to play an important role in county and national life, elsewhere sheep grazed amongst the decaying walls and ditches.

ABOVE:
Henry III (1216–72), who transformed the castle into a medieval palace; a portrait in stained glass from a 19th-century window at the east end of the Hall.

LEFT:
The castle as reconstructed by Henry III. The keep has gone and the Hall roof has been much altered. The castle's strengthened main gate and outer gate can be clearly seen in the far (west) wall.

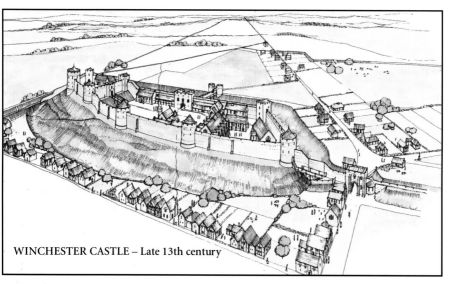

WINCHESTER CASTLE – Late 13th century

QUEEN ELEANOR'S GARDEN

In the 13th century King Henry III, his son Edward I and their wives, Eleanor of Provence and Eleanor of Castile, spent a great deal of time at Winchester Castle. Henry spent large amounts improving the accommodation within, creating a complex village of buildings around the Great Hall which he had built, interlinked by a network of sheltering alleyways. We know that within the walls there were at least three gardens (or 'herbaria'), although we do not know their location. It is likely that they were small oases of green tranquillity tucked away in odd spaces between the high walls of the grand buildings around.

Queen Eleanor's garden was created in 1986 and opened by HM Queen Elizabeth the Queen Mother as part of the Domesday Book 900th Anniversary celebrations. It shows what one such 'herber' might have looked like in about 1250–1300. The site to the south of the Great Hall would not always have been enclosed as it is now, but such a walled corner was typical of gardens of the period.

All the 80 or so plant varieties that grow there would have been seen in medieval gardens – the vine, the lily and the red and white rose as well as columbine, heartsease, vervain and many others with similarly beguiling names. Features such as the pool and the fountain with its bronze falcon have been meticulously created to match descriptions in historical records or to echo objects in nearby locations that date from the period in question. Other features such as the tunnel vine arbour and the trellised conversation area are copied from medieval illustrations.

ABOVE:
An illustration of a typical grand medieval lady in a garden, such as that recreated at Winchester Castle.

RIGHT:
Queen Eleanor's Garden, named after the wives of Henry III and Edward I.

FAR RIGHT:
The fountain in Queen Eleanor's garden. The design of its pedestal was based on that of a contemporary tomb at nearby St Cross Hospital.

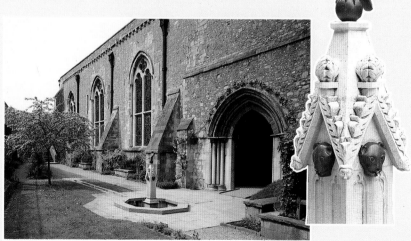

A Dream that Died

In the first years of the 17th century, the castle passed to a succession of private owners. In 1638 it was bestowed by Parliament on Sir William Waller, MP for Andover, who four years later sold the Great Hall to Hampshire's Justices of the Peace for the sum of £100.

Curiously, Waller was to play a large part in the castle's ultimate destruction. After the Civil War began in 1642, he became commander of the Parliamentary army in the south and west. Twice during the war, Royalist troops sought refuge in the castle from his Roundheads. On the first occasion in 1642 Waller flushed the King's men out by threatening to fire the main gate. But the following year Royalists retook the castle and for the next two years defied all the Parliamentarians' attempts to dislodge them.

In September 1645, Oliver Cromwell arrived in Winchester. Although the city surrendered quickly, the castle proved a much tougher nut to crack. For a week the Royalists, under Sir William Ogle, resisted all attempts to besiege it. In reply, Cromwell poured in a merciless barrage of cannon fire. After a week of terrifying bombardment and considerable damage to the entire fabric, the north wall was breached and Ogle surrendered. On 6 October, Cromwell and Waller entered the castle in triumph.

After this, Cromwell's Council of State resolved that Winchester Castle should never again be allowed to pose a threat, and in 1649 most of its remaining fortifications were pulled down. Waller's son sold the ruin to the city in 1656 for £260.

In 1651 King Charles II, as a young prince, had passed just south of Winchester on his meandering route towards a nine-year exile in France. Thirty-one years later, encouraged by the Corporation, he visited the area once more and was much impressed. The downs were ideal for hawking and hunting; the city was within a morning's ride of his beloved fleet at Portsmouth. Such was his enthusiasm that he determined to build there a summer palace in a spacious park. The city offered him the castle site and Sir Christopher Wren, architect of St Paul's Cathedral, was engaged to design the new palace.

Apart from the Great Hall, almost all traces of the old castle were erased, and over the next two years the palace grew, its progress keenly monitored by the king. It was built around three sides of a courtyard, open on the side facing the city. Wren's aim was to create a great vista stretching away to the cathedral, with terraces and steps leading to a grand avenue. The densely-packed houses that stood in the way were to be demolished. But it was not to be. In February 1685 the King died and work on the grand project was immediately halted, never to resume. But for Charles's untimely death the whole look of Winchester today would have been very different.

The empty shell of the King's House remained for a century and acted as a prison for many thousands of foreign soldiers during the Seven Years' War (1757–64) and the American War of Independence (1778–85). For some years it even accommodated 700 foreign clergy who had fled from the French Revolution.

In 1793, three years into the Napoleonic Wars, the house was bought by the army, becoming within a few years the main barracks of the south-west.

Over the next 50 years, levelling and construction on the site meant that most traces of the ancient castle and its ditches were eradicated.

In 1894, the King's House was destroyed by fire. The base is still visible from Queen Eleanor's Garden, complete with the marks of burning tar from the roof. Some of the ruined building's columns and façades were incorporated in the barrack blocks we see today, which remained in army use until 1983.

BELOW:
Winchester Castle and the King's House c.1795, looking to the south-west.

ABOVE:
King Charles II (1660–85). Successfully wooed by city authorities very keen to re-establish Winchester's royal connections, he visited the city to be made a Freeman in 1682. Following this, Charles commissioned a magnificent summer palace on the site of the castle. Only his death prevented its completion.

WINCHESTER CASTLE – Late 18th century

THE GREAT HALL

The Hall is generally acknowledged to be the finest surviving medieval aisled hall in England. It was built 1222–36 to replace the previous Norman hall, decorations being finished by Master Elias of Dereham, famed for his work on Salisbury Cathedral. The total cost was over £500.

The walls are made of flint, stone and rubble, and are largely as Elias would have seen them. The roof, though, has changed significantly. The original one was steeply pitched with nine dormer-style windows forming part of the walls. It was covered with shingles (oak tiles) and the eaves came down to a level about half-way down the present windows.

In the 14th century, probably during the reign of Richard II, the areas of the roof over the aisles were raised. The circles we see in the walls today are relocated remnants of the dormers. The lower tie beams of the roof were added as part of this work, to prevent further strain on the polished Purbeck stone pillars, which still have a marked lean. These tie-beams are the only elements of the medieval roof to have survived repairs carried out in the 19th century.

There were two large doors to the Hall. The south door that now leads to Queen Eleanor's garden once led to the inner bailey. Formerly this door had a large external porch. Over it were the king's apartments. Opposite was the north door, also with a porch. Although it was blocked off in 1789, traces of it can still be clearly seen today. Next to it, at the east end of the north wall, were two servants' doors to the kitchens and pantries.

The king would enter the Hall from the south door while the queen, it is thought, came through an elaborate marble doorway at the west end. They would sit on painted wooden thrones on a dais, probably at the west end of the Hall, where remains of a platform can still be seen. The solar, the royal family's private retiring chamber, was probably behind this. At the west end, about 6 feet (2m) up from the floor of the dais, a small channel passes obliquely through the wall. This was often thought to be 'the king's ear', a device by which the king could overhear the debates of his councillors without embarrassing them by his presence. Sadly, it is almost certain to be a 19th-century heating duct for the courts that sat here.

The window surrounds are a late and fine example of 'plate tracery', which involved carving the ornamental stonework from a single slab, as opposed to joining smaller pieces together. Originally, wooden shutters covered the

The east end of the Hall. The three kings in the lights above are, from left to right, William I, Stephen and Henry III. The stainless steel gates (1983) were designed and made by Antony Robinson, a gift of the people of Hampshire to commemorate the wedding of HRH The Prince of Wales to Lady Diana Spencer in July 1981. The painting on the east wall (1874) catalogues the county's parliamentary representatives from the time of Edward I. A blank scroll may mean that there was no representation in that year, or that the information was missing.

King Henry VIII (1509–47), almost certainly the monarch responsible for painting the Round Table prior to the visit of Charles V, the Holy Roman Emperor. For three centuries it had remained unadorned.

window spaces. During Henry III's alterations, frames were fitted in the main windows containing either glass or oiled paper. The lancet windows at the ends of the Hall are probably even earlier.

The walls were plastered and painted with pictures, patterns and coats of arms. Traces of this work are still visible. Around the Hall would have been a variety of adornments – statues in the porches, gilded heads over the royal dais, emblems and other embellishments painted on the doors.

In Henry III's time, the main decorative features were two paintings: at one end the Wheel of Fortune, a common 13th-century symbol; at the other the *Mappa Mundi*, a geographical chart of the world, a popular adornment of the time in the houses of the rich. The Round Table was probably there, but in an unpainted state.

A PLACE FOR JUSTICE

Throughout the Great Hall's long history, courts of law have been held here. Even kings, it was said, had to vacate the castle at times to make way for the Justices. At one end, the Quarter Sessions tried smaller criminal offences, referring more serious crimes to the Assizes which also sat there. At the other end sat a civil court, where individual grievances were tried.

Between 1871 and 1874 the building was extended to the east. Judges and Justices now processed through the Great Hall to new court rooms built on the site of the ancient castle ditch. The Round Table was moved to the west end to make way for a through doorway in what was formerly the outer wall of the castle. Fifty feet (15m) high, this wall proved to be 10 feet (3m) thick with no foundation!

There followed a complete reroofing and restoration of the Hall. The windows were reglazed with the coats of arms of kings, noblemen and clergy who had links with the county or the castle. Around the arch to the courts, in a great tree, were painted the names of Hampshire's parliamentary representatives from the time of Edward I.

ABOVE:
The Hall pre-1974 in its role as a court. The last trial held here was that of the Price sisters, convicted of IRA terrorism in 1973.

ABOVE INSET:
The Judges' bench against the north wall. Nearby, the entrance to the late 18th-century holding cells is still in evidence in the floor.

LEFT:
The statue of Queen Victoria (1887) by Sir Alfred Gilbert (sculptor of Eros in Piccadilly Circus). First in Castle Yard, it was dismantled in 1892 because it obstructed the judges' carriages and the light to the County Council offices. After a spell near the Guildhall it was re-erected in the Hall and unveiled for a second time in 1910.

From the earliest days of the Victorian court buildings, cracks had begun to appear in the walls. By 1938 the situation had become critical, and the courts were forced to make a hasty return to the Great Hall. Only after new courts were opened in 1974 could the Hall once more resume its ancient appearance. In 1975–76 Hampshire County Council carried out a major restoration of the Hall, which is now maintained by the County Council as an important national monument. The Great Hall still serves as the symbolic centre for the county's administration, as it has for so long. The County Council's headquarters are even today known as The Castle.

The Hall still hosts ceremonial occasions. In 1979, Her Majesty The Queen attended a Maundy Thursday lunch, dining at a newly-created Round Table. In July 1992 Rouge Croix Pursuivant of Arms presented Hampshire County Council with its grant of arms there. In the same month, the Princess of Wales attended a reception in the Hall to bid farewell to the Royal Hampshire Regiment when it amalgamated with the Queen's Regiment.

The castle dungeons played host to many important prisoners and public executions were commonplace. In 1330 Edmund, Earl of Kent, was tried and condemned to death for conspiracy by Parliament sitting in the Great Hall. After a day's wait, he was executed at the gate by a fellow prisoner. In 1603, the Plague raging in London caused the Law Courts to be transferred to Winchester. As a result Sir Walter Raleigh and his companions were tried in the Hall for plotting against the Crown. In the face of provocation Raleigh bore himself with great dignity. Although condemned to death, he survived for a further 14 years.

Following the unsuccessful rebellion of 1685 led by the Duke of Monmouth, the infamous Lord Chief Justice, Judge Jeffreys, opened the Commission in the Great Hall. He unashamedly bullied the jury into condemning to death Alice Lisle, widow of a New Forest landowner, for harbouring rebel fugitives. Jeffreys wanted her to be burned on the afternoon of her conviction. All that the vociferous protest of local people could achieve was a five-day delay and a commutation of the sentence to beheading.

LEFT:
A portrait of Sir Walter Raleigh. In 1603 he was charged in the castle with plotting against James I, and condemned to death. He was saved by a last minute reprieve, only to be executed a few years later in the Tower of London.

RIGHT:
A modern view of the Castle. The 18th-century barrack buildings are prominent to the left, where King's House once stood, with County Council buildings on the right. The 1974 Law Courts dominate the Great Hall in the centre foreground. The ancient castle earthworks have disappeared. Little but the Hall and Westgate survive from the days of the great palace fortress.

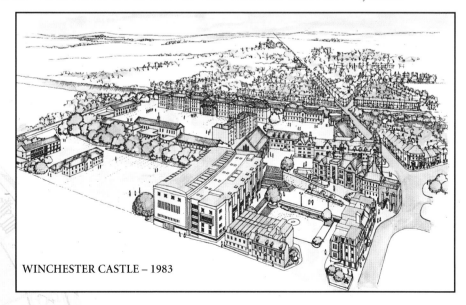

WINCHESTER CASTLE – 1983

THE ROUND TABLE AND THE ARTHURIAN LEGEND

The Round Table is 18 feet (5.5m) in diameter, weighs 1.2 tons and contains 121 pieces of oak from at least seven trees. The surface is formed by 51 thin wedge-shaped planks. The table has hung in Winchester since medieval times and has probably always been in the Hall. It does not date from the 5th or 6th century, when Arthur is traditionally supposed to have fought the Anglo-Saxon invaders. Both carbon-dating and examination of the tree rings during the table's restoration in 1976 confirm that it was made between 1250 and 1280, most probably in the earlier part of the reign of King Edward I (1272–1307), when the age of chivalry was at its height. Indeed, Edward was known for his great interest in the Arthurian legend. In 1278 both he and his queen were present at Glastonbury Abbey when tombs thought to be those of Arthur and Guinevere were opened.

The 1976 tests also proved almost certainly that what we see today **was** originally a table. Mortice holes in each of the 12 radial 'spokes' on the back of the table show where 12 legs were broken off when it was hung. At the same time, vertical timbers were roughly nailed on the back and a raised rim was added to the front to prevent distortion.

The table was unpainted when it was originally hung. The reason for display-ing a plain wooden disc can only have been that the table was already by then firmly associated with King Arthur. The canopy over the king indicates that it was painted in the 16th century, probably for King Henry VIII when he brought Charles V, the newly crowned Holy Roman Emperor, to view the table in 1522. It was repainted in 1789 to the same design by William Cave, a local artist. X-rays show that what Charles saw was a likeness of the young, bearded Henry, a neat way of reinforcing Henry's claim to the inheritance of the British kings and an authority derived through Arthur from Constantine the Great.